# FOOTBALL RISING STARS

First published in the UK by Sweet Cherry Publishing Limited, 2023
Unit 36, Vulcan House, Vulcan Road,
Leicester, LE5 3EF, United Kingdom

Sweet Cherry Europe (Europe address)
Nauschgasse 4/3/2 POB 1017
Vienna, WI 1220, Austria

2 4 6 8 10 9 7 5 3 1

ISBN: 978-1-80263-094-7

Football Rising Stars: Leah Williamson

Text by Harry Meredith
Illustrations by Sophie Jones

www.sweetcherrypublishing.com

Printed and bound in India

# LEAH WILLIAMSON

**THE UNOFFICIAL STORY**

Written by
## HARRY MEREDITH

Sweet Cherry

# CONTENTS

# ENGLAND'S PRIDE

Thousands of fans lined the streets as the England team arrived at Wembley Stadium. Leah Williamson, England's women's national team captain, looked out of the coach window. Faces were painted red and white, flags bellowed in the gentle summer

breeze and the atmosphere was buzzing with excitement and hope.

Leah spotted a young girl, wearing a full kit and a bucket hat, sitting on the shoulders of her father. The girl was clapping and cheering as her heroes passed. The Lionesses had sparked joy across the nation. Even those not normally interested in men's football, couldn't help but be caught up in the excitement. There was something special about this team; something huge, in fact. The only way someone might not have heard of The Lionesses was if they'd been holed up in a cellar away from the social media, internet, newspapers, magazines, television and the radio. It was almost impossible to open a paper or turn on the TV without seeing something about them. Leah and the rest of the team had blasted the cobwebs out of women's football. They'd started an incredible journey and managed to take the whole country right along with them. Leah and the rest of the England team had changed the game forever.

Right now, the country was united in anticipation of the biggest football match of the summer. It was the decisive stop of the tournament. The Lionesses were playing in the UEFA Women's Euro 2022 Final at Wembley Stadium, in front of a record-breaking crowd of 87,192 people.

The coach pulled up by the players' entrance. Sarina Wiegman, the England manager, left the coach first. Leah and the other players followed closely behind. This was the moment that they had dreamed of. Now it was finally happening.

Leah wasn't usually much of a smiler pre-match, but today she just couldn't help it. From the corridor, the players made their way to the changing rooms. Leah spotted her shirt hanging up in its usual place and made her way over to her seat. She felt immense pride each time she saw the captain's armband neatly placed by her shorts, shin pads and socks.

Inside the changing room, Leah's specially created playlist was on full blast. The music included Beyonce's

*Break My Soul* and Celine Dion's version of *River Deep, Mountain High*. These were songs that kept the team's spirits up and ready for what lay ahead.

With this match, the world was becoming aware of women's football. But right now, all Leah wanted was for the crowd to have just as good a time as the England team.

Leah led the team into the tunnel. Only a handful of years ago, Leah was playing football on parks, muddy pitches and indoor sports halls.

Now she was leading her nation out as captain in the UEFA Women's Euro 2022 Final.

It was time to make history.

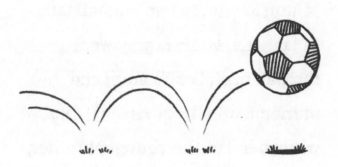

# 2
# MILTON KEYNES

Football was in Leah's blood. She was born on the 29th of March 1997 in Milton Keynes to two football fans. In fact, her whole family were football mad. Leah's mum and grandma were huge Arsenal fans, while her dad and younger brother,

Jacob, supported Tottenham Hotspur.

Leah's mum had played football herself when she young. Because of these hard experiences, she was nervous for her daughter to play football, as she understood what Leah would be signing herself up for. Back in the 1980s, girls didn't have as many opportunities to play football and attitudes were different. It was tough in school too. During sports lessons at school, teachers made girls play netball, while boys played football. During playtimes, boys chased balls around the playground, and if girls wanted to join in, they were made fun of.

Back in 1921, the Football Association decided that women should be banned from playing football in league stadiums. The ban ended in 1971, but girls playing football still wasn't taken seriously or encouraged. Women's football matches weren't shown on television until Channel 4 started airing coverage in 1989, and even then, it was only once a year for the Women's FA Cup Final.

So, it was no wonder that getting into football was a struggle for Leah.

Six-year-old Leah was really into gymnastics. She loved the way it let her release all her energy by spinning, rolling and jumping around. At the end of one of her gym classes, the coach threw a ball towards everyone. It was just a bit of fun, but it was a moment that changed Leah's life forever. Most of the other girls ran away from the ball, but Leah gave the ball a good kick and was instantly hooked. After class, Leah returned  home with a smile beaming from her face and a newfound passion.

Leah loved football, and she asked her mum if she would be able to help her join a team.

Football might not have been seen as a good fit for girls, but Leah's parents were determined things would be different for their daughter. After all, why shouldn't girls play football? Why shouldn't they be just as good as boys? Surely someone like Leah, who had so much talent and determination, could get involved in the game?

# 3

# SCOTS SPORTS & SOCIAL CLUB

Leah's mum spoke to the coach of Scot Youth, a local team made up of boys. He agreed to let Leah come along to a practice. When she arrived, the coach told Leah he wasn't going

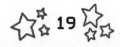

to give her any special treatment
just because she was a girl. If she
didn't have the skills, she wouldn't be
allowed to join the team.

The coach introduced Leah to the
team and the training started. Leah
jogged, jumped and stretched before
taking part in training drills. She
zipped and zoomed between cones,
passed the ball and worked on her
touch. Then, it was time for a practice
match. Two players were chosen as
captains, and they took it in turns
to pick their teams. Leah's name
was the last to be called. Gutted, but

determined not to let it affect her, Leah walked over to her team with her head held high. The two teams went into their separate halves and the coach threw a ball onto the pitch.

Leah's team won the ball. Her teammate ignored Leah and passed it to another player. When the other team grabbed the ball, Leah immediately raced over and stole it back, running past a defender before passing it to her teammate. He pulled back his right foot and fired the ball into the net.

It was obvious that Leah was more than good enough. In fact, she was one of the best players Scot Youth had ever seen. Leah soon became their star striker.

But even this wasn't enough for some supporters who just couldn't understand why a girl was playing at all. Leah didn't let this negativity get to her. The year at Scot Youth made her a stronger person and player. Her best revenge was making sure she won every game.

After a year, Leah had a lot of experience under her belt, and her raw talent had been sharpened through endless football matches.

Now it was time to get serious.
Leah moved on to AFC Rushden &
Diamonds, a football academy run by
the football club of the same name.

Leah trained, learned and played
as hard as she could. And it didn't
go unnoticed. When her coach was
offered a role at Arsenal, she told
them all about the talented nine-
year-old player who seemed destined
for a career in football, and Leah was
offered a trial for the under 10s.

It was a huge opportunity. As
 Leah walked into the
stadium with her mum

and dad, she couldn't help but panic
that her nerves would get the better
of her. But she needn't have worried.
She knew the football pitch like the
back of hand after years of watching
Arsenal play at home with her mum
and grandma. It felt like coming
home, and Leah felt her nerves slip
away as she gave the trials everything
she had.

Straight after the trials, Leah was
called into an academy office to speak
with her coach and the academy
director. Her heart was beating out of
her chest as she walked inside. Had

she done enough to showcase her talent? Leah looked straight at her coach, who was trying, but failing miserably to hide a huge smile. Leah's heart leapt.

It was happening, it was really happening.

At the age of nine-years-old, Leah Williamson was going to be an Arsenal Academy player.

# 4
# STARTING AT ARSENAL

Leah and her parents were invited to a special evening at the academy where all the U10s players could meet each other. The coaches wanted to make sure that everyone felt like they belonged and that their parents knew they would be looked after properly.

The coaches welcomed everyone
to the event. They made it clear to
Leah and the other young players
that although everyone in the room
was incredibly talented, they needed
to give everything they had every
single day. With the coaches help,
some of them could go on to become
professional footballers. Leah was
determined that she would be one
of them.

Leah could hardly believe
her eyes as they were given
a tour around the academy.
There were indoor and

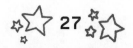

outdoor pitches, as well as classrooms and treatment rooms. Everything and more that Leah could possibly need. All she had to think about now was one thing; football.

At the end of the evening, Leah was handed a large bag. Her eyes lit up as she realised what was inside; new football kits! When Leah had taken part in her initial trials with Arsenal, she was one of the only children playing in their own training gear. In the bag given to her by the academy, there were tops, shorts and socks.

The home kit, away kit and all of the latest clothes. But Leah's enthusiasm swiftly faded as she noticed the number on the back of her shirt. Like the rest of the young players, she was desperate for one of the iconic numbers like 7, 8, 9 and 10. To wear the famous numbers worn by Arsenal legends such as Ian Wright, Kelly Smith and Dennis Bergkamp. Leah was gutted that she'd been given the number 6.

Her mum and dad immediately saw how disappointed Leah was, so they hatched a plan. They went out and bought her some expensive football trainers. These weren't any old trainers, but black with a red logo, and had the stitching of her initials followed by the number six. From this moment onwards the number six became Leah's lucky number. It had started as something she didn't like but would become a number she would cherish and make her own.

Above all, her parents' kindness made her realise just how much her family believed in her. And for that, Leah was going to do everything within her power to succeed.

She would make the most of her opportunity to play and impress in a professional academy. Leah was determined not to let them down.

# 5

# ACADEMY LIFE

In order to succeed at the academy, Leah had to dedicate herself entirely to football. There was no time to relax or take things easy as every minute counted. While it was an incredibly exciting time, it was also tough as not all the players would go on to become

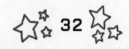

professional players. Thousands of talented players make it into academy programmes, but there is only a certain amount of professional football players. Unfortunately, some just wouldn't be good enough. Every year, new players joined the team and others were let go.

There were late nights, early mornings, travelling, not to mention trying to balance schoolwork and never having time to see friends.

 But Leah had exactly the right attitude. She was happy to give up things that other kids her age were doing. She had chosen to trade parties for training drills, video games for laps around the pitch and shopping trips for muscle recovery.

Leah had exactly what it takes: dedication, team spirit and most of all a positive attitude. Her determination and talent shone through, and she made her way up in the academy year-after-year, getting better and better at every stage.

But as she approached her GCSEs, the pressure suddenly felt too much, and Leah was hit by doubt. She was

already struggling to balance her schoolwork with playing football. The pressure felt unbearable.

 In the men's game, professional football players can earn huge amounts of money. But sadly, the same couldn't be said for the women's game. Most female football players had to work a full-time job as well as play to make a living. How would she cope if she had to get a job to support herself and play as well? Would Leah really be able to juggle it all?

She decided to talk to her dad about how she was feeling. Leah's parents had always been her biggest fans and were always there to make her feel better no matter what. Almost as soon as Leah had finished speaking, her dad gave her a huge hug.

'One day, Leah, football will be your job,' he told her, reminding her just how far the women's game had come, and that by the time Leah was a professional player she would hopefully make enough money through football. He also pointed out how the game desperately needed more players like Leah.

Thanks to her dad's wise words, Leah realised she didn't need to worry so much. Whatever happened, happened. Right now, she loved football with her whole being, and everything else she could figure out with the help of her family and her coach.

Soon after, Leah's hard work paid off. Shelly Kerr, the Arsenal manager, pulled her to one side and gave her the news she'd been waiting her whole life to hear. Leah was going to play for the first team.

It had taken seven years of giving everything she had to the academy, but as Leah wiped tears of happiness from her eyes, she knew without doubt that every single moment had been worth it.

# 6
# EARNING HER SHIRT

One of Leah's most precious

possessions was a signed photo from

her hero, Kelly Smith. Smith was

an Arsenal and England striker and

England's second highest scorer.

Across the top of the photo, Kelly

had scrawled the words 'Dream big!';

a phrase that Leah whispered to herself whenever she looked at the photo. Now Leah's dream of playing on Arsenal's first team was not only coming true, she was also about to play on the same team as Smith.

It was 30th March 2014, and Arsenal were facing Birmingham City in the quarter-final of the Champions League. The match was being played at The Hive, the home of Barnet FC. For most of the game Leah was on the bench. She watched on eagerly as the minutes ticked, hoping she might get to play. The match wasn't going well for Arsenal. In fact, they were losing 0-2 thanks to a pair of quickfire goals from Birmingham City's Kirsty Linnett and Remi Allen.

With only a handful of minutes left to play, the Arsenal manager told Leah warm up. She quickly tied and untied her laces three times to try and get rid of her nerves. Before she knew it, Leah was heading onto the pitch, substituting for the Arsenal legend Rachel Yankey. Leah wanted to pinch herself. When she was younger, Leah had Yankey's name on the back of one of her tops. Now she was taking her place.

But there was no time to think about that. The 17-year-old Leah burst onto the pitch full of energy and worked as hard as she could. At the end of the game, Arsenal may not have won, but Leah had fully gained the respect of her teammates.

Leah's star was rising quickly. Shortly afterwards, she made her FA Women's Super League debut on April 16th, 2014, against Notts County.

Leah was also included in the squad for the FA Cup final against Everton. This match was extra-special as it was held in Leah's hometown of Milton Keynes. Almost 100 of Leah's friends and family came to cheer her on as Arsenal defeated Everton 2-0 in the match and became the champions of the FA Cup.

At the final whistle, Leah searched for her family in the crowd. They were pretty easy to find as her mum's voice could be heard from the side-lines no matter how loud the rest of the fans were chanting. Her whole family were on their feet, cheering and celebrating. As Leah collected her medal and lifted her first-ever trophy with the team, she felt like she was floating on air.

After twelve appearances in the 2014 Women's Super League, reaching the Women's Super League FA Cup final and helping Arsenal win the League Cup, Leah signed her first professional contract with Arsenal. All the hard work had been worth it, all her dreams of becoming a professional footballer player were finally coming true. Not only that,

but the 18-year-old was also awarded the PFA Young Women's Player of the Year Award. It was clear that Leah's huge talent wasn't just being taken seriously by her team, but by the football community as well. Everyone was waiting to see what she did next.

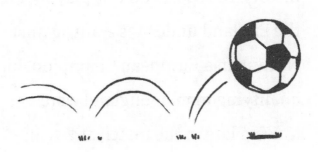

# 7
# THE PENALTY

Then came the worst moment of Leah's career, as well as one of the most unusual incidents in football history. In 2015, Leah was playing for the England under 19s team against Norway in a European Championship qualifying match. England were trailing late in the match at 2-1.

But they had earned an injury-time penalty in the 96th minute. As England's nominated penalty taker, it was up to Leah to get the job done.

Determined not to let the pressure of taking the penalty get to her, Leah focused her mind, stepped up to the ball and fired the ball into the net. Her teammates went wild; Leah had scored the winning goal that would take her team through to the tournament. But things were not as rosy they appeared.

The referee blew her whistle, saying that Leah's teammate Rosella Ayane had broken the rules by entering the penalty box around the goal while Leah was taking the penalty. The goal was disallowed, and the referee gave a free kick to Norway. England had lost the game.

After the final whistle, just sixteen seconds later, Pat Frost, who was in charge of England's equipment, ran onto the pitch to tell Leah that she had been cheated. The referee hadn't followed the rules which said that Leah should have been allowed to retake the penalty. None of the team could believe what had happened, and they weren't going to let it go without a fight. They went straight to the European football's governing body, UEFA.

Representatives at UEFA later reviewed the footage from the match and decided that the wrong decision had been made by the referee. They ruled that England's game against Norway would start again from the minute the penalty kick was awarded to England. The referee was sent home from the tournament, and a

new one brought in instead.

Nothing like this had ever happened before in football. It was unbelievable. As soon as head coach Mo Marley heard UEFA's decision, she sent for Leah. Leah was trying to relax in the bath in her hotel room at the time and immediately jumped out and ran downstairs with wet hair. Leah was so shocked that she passed out on her way back to her hotel room.

Everyone could see that Leah was scared stiff of messing up the penalty. She didn't want to let her team or her country down. But the rest of the team did everything they could to let her know that they believed in her and couldn't think of anyone better to take the shot.

Before the penalty could be taken, there was the small matter of their upcoming game against Switzerland. That match was played on the same day as the penalty retake. And with that game came yet another twist. With the score at 1-1, England were awarded another penalty, and Leah had to step up to take the shot. Leah was determined not to miss, she wanted to make sure that the Norwegian team, particularly the goalkeeper, were kept on edge for the penalty retake later that night. Pushing everything else out of her mind, Leah stepped up, took aim and watched in relief as the goal flew straight into the goal. England won the match.

Finally, that evening it was time for the penalty retake against Norway. The England coach pulled up to a horde of cameras waiting for a glimpse of Leah. The event had turned into a huge news story. Bets were being made on the outcome, broadcasters were televising the live event, and local people had turned up to be a part of football history. Leah grabbed an ice box and stepped off the coach, trying to hide behind some of the other players. Once inside the changing room, she put on a playlist she'd created specially which included the track *End Credits* by Chase & Status featuring Plan B, determined to lose herself in the music.

Despite her best efforts, Leah's anxiety started to take over and she

burst into tears. Her teammate, Katie Zelm, hurried over and gave her a huge hug. The whole team quickly followed and gathered around her. They made it clear that whatever the outcome they were behind her and there was no one they trusted more. She was someone they had complete faith in. But did Leah believe that? Could she overcome one of the most high-pressure moments of her career?

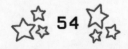

# 8
# LEAH'S NERVES

The team did everything they could to keep Leah's nerves in check. Marley made sure they warmed up like they would for a ninety-minute match. Then it was back into the changing room and into the tunnel alongside the Norwegians. The Norway players

tried their best to get into Leah's head, laughing and pointing at her as she stood in the line of England players. Leah took no notice and focussed on the job in hand instead. Head held high; she led the team onto the same field on which they had beaten Switzerland a few hours earlier. Everyone took their positions at the same end the penalty had happened.

Leah placed the ball on the pitch, but the Norwegian goalkeeper complained about its positioning, trying to make Leah even more nervous. Leah placed it down

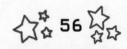

again, stepped forward then kicked it straight past the goalkeepers outstretched right hand and into the goal. Leah had done it.

There was still sixteen seconds of the game remaining. Somehow, Leah and the rest of the England team managed to stay calm. Those final few moments seemed to last an age before the replacement referee, Kateryna Zora, blew her whistle for full time. England had qualified for the summer's U19 European Championships.

Leah dropped to her knees in half-exhaustion and half-celebration, before finding her mum. The two hugged each other and cried with joy.

With the relief of winning both matches, the team celebrated all night. But when they finally got home, Leah couldn't switch off her anxiety. As her teammate Gabby was fast asleep in the room they were sharing, Leah went into the bathroom and laid on the floor, looking at her phone. She used the ball she'd scored the penalty with as a pillow.

The next day, Leah made a decision.

She knew she couldn't carry on with the anxiety. In every match, she secretly worried that she wasn't as good a footballer as everyone thought and that it was only a matter of time before she was found out. So Leah took control and arranged therapy sessions with the Arsenal and England psychologist, Katie Green.

Green's approach, which included breathing exercises, had Leah feeling back on form within a fortnight. Taking her mental health seriously was the best decision Leah made. She never kept it a secret and made

sure to talk about her struggles in case it helped someone else reach out for support.

Leah was about to need every single one of the tools that Green had given her, as in the summer of 2018, the national team manager Phil Neville, asked Leah to make her senior team debut.

Leah was over the moon. And her dad was too; he joked that he could finally support his daughter's team. Her dad was always thrilled that his daughter had made it as a professional football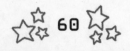

player, but as Tottenham Hotspur fan, it took a while to get used to seeing his daughter in an Arsenal shirt. Now she'd be playing in the famous lioness kit!

Leah met up with her fellow Lionesses' and they travelled to Moscow where England were playing away in a FIFA Women's World Cup qualifier against Russia. Leah wasn't the only Arsenal player travelling, as Jordan Nobbs and Beth Mead were also part of the England setup.

England players were given a shirt number based on where they're playing. A right-sided centre back is 5 and the left side is 6. For Leah's first senior start, she was due to be playing on the right side but for some reason Leah was given the number 6. She couldn't believe it. Surely, this had to be a good sign.

It turned out to be exactly that. In the final six minutes of the game, Leah was sent on as a substitute for Keira Walsh. Leah worked hard during her short debut and England won the match 1-3.

The England manager, Phil Neville, received message after message from supporters who wanted to see more of Leah. The fans were excited to see what Leah could do in an England shirt. Leah's career wasn't only on the up, but it was about to move up another notch entirely.

# 9

# WSL CHAMPIONS

Joe Montemurro was named as the new manager of Arsenal in 2017. He had been a fan of Arsenal since he was a child, so it was a dream come true for him to manage them. More than anything, he was determined to get them into shape.

He knew that there was change happening in women's football. Clubs were starting to put more money into them, and he didn't want Arsenal to fall behind. Teams such as Chelsea and Manchester City had been progressing and often finishing their seasons with silverware. Arsenal struggled to catchup with these breakaway teams. Something had to change, and the club hoped that new investment and a new manager was the answer.

Leah immediately loved her new manager's style. Montemurro was incredibly clear about how he wanted the team to play and was also one of the most laid-back coaches that the team had ever worked for. He wanted to play a type of football that heavily relied on the team's defenders being skilled with the ball at their feet. He also taught the players to focus on what they could do with the ball rather than thinking about winning trophies and games. If they could control the game when they had the ball and be proactive when defending, they would win. With this approach it wasn't long before Leah and the rest of the team began to improve.

Montemurro wanted Leah to start playing as a centre-back. At first Leah was taken aback by this request. But Leah was ready to do anything for her team and embraced the change. As a young player, she needed someone to guide her and to help her develop. Montemurro was that someone. During training, he had identified that Leah had the abilities he wanted in a centre back. Her combative style, alongside her composure and passing ability, was the perfect blend for his new look Arsenal.

Leah took the positional move in her stride and quickly became a fan favourite as Arsenal turned into a strong force in the Women's Super League. Win after win after win followed. Vivienne Miedema couldn't stop scoring, Mead couldn't stop assisting and Leah couldn't stop defending. The whole team was on fire. Fans and critics fell in love with the football they were playing.

Arsenal were soon taking over the league. But despite sweeping everyone aside with ease, it was still a

rollercoaster season, as they suffered a mid-season injury crisis with player after player getting hurt.

For Leah, it was hard to watch her friends get injured. When Nobbs tore her knee, Leah struggled to keep her emotions in check. She understood what it meant to play, and to someone have that taken away by an injury was heartbreaking. Not only that, but Leah also cared for her teammates as people. She didn't see them as just teammates or colleagues, but as lifelong friends that she wanted the best for.

In this scenario, many teams would crumble, but Arsenal defied the odds and kept their run going. They had to dig deep, stick together and continue to grind out results. Arsenal had a chance to win the trophy in front of a record-breaking crowd. They had earned an incredible opportunity to claim Arsenal's first Women's Super League title for seven years.

For this crucial match, Arsenal's opponents were Brighton and Hove Albion. Despite the distance between the clubs, hundreds of fans had travelled to Brighton to have a chance of witnessing their team be crowned as champions. On the day, Leah and her team did not let those who had travelled down. The team put on a strong-willed performance, running riot with a 0-4 victory. With goals from Miedema, Katie McCabe, Mead and Daniëlle van de Donk. At the end of the match, Leah and her teammates all ran into a circle on the pitch, jumping up and down to celebrate what they had just achieved.

As soon as she could, Leah ran to her family and sobbed her heart out as her mum hugged her. The clip was shared around the world and went viral. Everyone appreciated the pure joy and raw emotion on display. It was clear to all just how much this meant to not only Arsenal, but to Leah. She was Arsenal through and through.

There was no doubt that Leah was winning hearts around the nation. But there was no time to relax, as the following week there was still one more game to play to complete the season. Arsenal might have won the trophy, but the upcoming match would serve a different purpose. It would prove Arsenal's place as

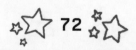

undisputed champions.

During the league campaign, Manchester City had been the closest challengers to the title. In fact, going into the final game of the season, they had yet to lose in the league. Arsenal had won the trophy because they'd won all their other matches and drawn none. Manchester City, on the other hand, had drawn five and won the other fourteen. Arsenal was ahead with an unbeatable four points on the final day of the season.

On the day of the match, the Manchester City players lined up by the tunnel and clapped Arsenal as they walked onto the pitch. A football tradition, where after a team has won the league, opposition teams have the choice to offer a guard of honour to the league victors. But that was when any niceness ended. Manchester City wanted to have an unbeaten season and were determined to win.

The match was being played in front of a sell-out crowd at home. It was clear that Arsenal were up for the fight, but so were Manchester City who had the first shot at

goal, the ball narrowly bouncing past the post. Arsenal then had one of their own goal attempts stopped by Ellie Roebuck, the Manchester City goalkeeper. More chances followed, but the deadlock seemed unbreakable. Leah and her teammates managed to keep Manchester City at bay, but no matter how hard the Arsenal attackers tried it appeared that there was no way to get past Roebuck.

Finally, in the 88th minute, Arsenal came up with something special.

After a corner, the ball bounced out to Leah who headed it down to her teammates. Emma Mukandi brought the ball under her control and fired a rocket of a shot at the goal which flew straight into the back of the net. Leah and the rest of her teammates ran to Mukandi to celebrate. Moments later, the referee brought the whistle to her lips and the match and season was over. Arsenal had proved just why they were the 2018/2019 Women's Super League champions.

The trophy was brought out onto the pitch, as were the medals, which

were handed out to all of the players.
As Leah was handed hers, she couldn't
stop smiling. Arsenal had really done
it. They were league champions!

# 10
# THE ARMBAND

The talent and skill that Leah had shown at Arsenal meant that she was chosen as a member of the squad for the 2019 World Cup. She was one of the youngest in the team and was heading into the tournament with the expectation that she might not

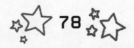

get to play much. But this wasn't
going to stop Leah from enjoying the
remarkable opportunity. Football
players across the world dream
of getting the chance to play for
their country in an international
tournament. And Leah wasn't just
going to dream about it, she was
going to live it.

Leah and the rest of the team were
determined to make the most of their
time in France. The older Lionesses
told Leah and the younger players
to have fun and to make as many
memories as possible. Reminding

them that later in their career they might not have the same freedom.

Leah made sure she enjoyed the sunshine. She went outside a lot and skimmed stones on the dazzling beach front in Nice. She also made constant use of her 35mm camera. Leah always made sure to take this camera everywhere she goes and did her best to capture each and every moment. She wanted photographs so she could remember and cherish every memory. She made sure to take photos of the day she, Walsh and Georgia

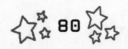

Stanway rented electric scooters to explore France. The three young players raced through their beautiful surroundings. The sun on their backs, wind in their hair and smiles beaming across their faces. The trio didn't want to waste a single moment.

Back on the pitch, England made it all the way to the semi-finals. Yet sadly, the Lionesses lost 2-1 against the USA in a closely fought encounter and were eliminated. As expected, Leah watched most of the matches from the bench, aching to get out onto the pitch, but she did get to make her World Cup debut in a group stage match against Cameroon.

Playing such a small part of the World Cup had left Leah frustrated and wanting more. She felt her progress was too slow, and she longed to show what she was capable of.

A few months later in winter, in an international friendly match against the Czech Republic, Leah got the chance to do exactly that. In the 86th minute the two sides were head-to-head. The match was locked at 2-2 with only a few minutes remaining. England had a corner and Leah stood

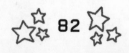

at the edge of the box. The ball swung into the box, swerving past the falling snowflakes, and was headed away by a defender. The ball fell at Leah's feet.

She shifted her body and fired

a shot at the goal. The ball flew past a crowded penalty area, hitting an outstretched defender's leg before nestling into the bottom left corner of the net.

Leah had scored her first ever England goal and had set her team on the way to a win in the closing minutes of the match.

Leah was finally starting to feel like a valued and essential member of the national team setup. She'd won the league with Arsenal, scored for England and had truly earned her place with some brilliant performances.

On March 14th 2020, everything came crashing to a halt. The entire world was stopped in its tracks. The COVID-19 virus had arrived and forced everyone into lockdown.

 There was no more football, matches or tournaments.

Everyone's lives had to change due to the world-wide pandemic.

Everything Leah loved was put on hold. Not only that, it felt as if women's football didn't exist. Before the pandemic, it was riding high, but now it was as if they didn't matter. The men's teams began playing again on June 17th and lots of money had been invested in to make sure the Premier League and FA Cup matches were safe. But the women's matches were kept on hold. It felt as if women's football was once again being dismissed.

For Leah, this was about women having the freedom to be able to do what they want in any walk of life. Sport was an amazing way to show that women can play just as well as the men. Leah wanted football to show this. It was so important that she didn't lose the ground they had made.

Frustrated, Leah and her housemate and fellow player, Nobbs, kept on top of their fitness with a home strength and conditioning programme. Leah also decided to learn the piano, dedicating at least ten minutes a day to her new hobby.

She also went out of her way to look out for her teammates during lockdown. Both Miedema and Lisa Evans were stuck in Scotland, so every day, Leah would make sure to walk by their house in England and check their post. The whole team could see that Leah was someone they could rely on – she was a leader both on and off the pitch.

In July, the FA finally decided to let matches restart with the new league and the final rounds of the postponed 2020 FA Women's Cup in September.

Leah was chosen to be a member

of Team GB at the rearranged Tokyo Olympics. She flew out to Japan with a new set of teammates and got ready to make her Olympic debut. There were no fans inside stadiums because of pandemic rules and her family weren't allowed to travel to Japan. But it still meant everything to Leah. In 2012, she had watched the London Olympics in awe and knew what it would mean to be an Olympian. Nine years later she was exactly that.

Leah had to hold back tears of joy as she stood proudly by her teammates as the national anthem was played before matches. Sadly, England were knocked out at the quarter-final stage against a tough Australian side. Despite a hat-trick from striker Ellen White, the Aussies won the match 4-3 in extra time. But Leah herself shone, starring in the centre of defence. Team GB might not have won a medal, but Leah had taken Tokyo and the rest of the watching football world by storm.

Towards the end of 2021, England needed to name a new manager. Phil Neville was leaving to take over at Inter Miami, the newly created team

setup by David Beckham. Sarina Wiegman took over as the new England manager. Wiegman had led The Netherlands to their UEFA Euro success in 2017. Could she help England do the same?

Leah was sad to see Neville go, but she couldn't help but be excited about her new boss. Wiegman appeared smart and well mannered and she commanded respect from everyone in the team without forcing it. The players were slightly on edge as they wanted to impress her and earn their spot on the team.

Wiegman was impressed with how Leah had progressed over the years, both physically and mentally. She saw that Leah had made the transition from fledgling youngster to an established member of the squad. A player that was no longer a bench warmer, but one of the first names on the team sheet.

As well as taking over the team, Wiegman had an incredibly important decision to make. Steph Houghton was a huge part of England's defence and was the national team's captain. But Steph

was currently unable to play due to
a torn Achilles tendon. She still had
a long recovery ahead of her before
she could be match-ready again.
There was no way Houghton could be
Captain right now.

During the first day of camp,
Wiegman asked Leah if she had five
minutes to spare. Leah immediately
thought she was in trouble. Her
mind started running through all
the things she might have done, but
she couldn't come up with anything.
Leah had no idea that the manager
had pulled her to one side to ask her

a question only a handful of special football players have ever been asked.

'How would you like to be England captain?' Sarina asked Leah.

Leah's first reaction was to laugh. She couldn't believe it. Then after the laughter, Leah was overwhelmed with gratitude. This was one of the biggest honours of her life.

Somehow, Leah pulled herself together, took a deep breath and replied with the only answer she could ever imagine giving.

'*Yes.*'

And with that, Leah added her name to a famous list. Alongside the likes of Bobby Moore, Casey Stoney, David Beckham and Steph Houghton.

Leah Williamson was now England's captain.

# 11
# EURO 2022

The Lionesses, with their new captain Leah, were heading into the summer tournament full of hope. Wiegman had brought an exciting brand of football to the team, and they were putting on an impressive show which was pulling in fans in the stadiums and at home watching on TV.

A win in the newly formed Arnold Clark Cup, where Germany, Spain, Canada and England – four of the world's top 10 nations – played round-robin matches, had shown that England were one of the best national teams in the world.

Leah believed England had a great chance of winning the European Championship on their home turf but was still expected to be tested at every match. More than anything, she wanted the Lionesses to inspire young women and girls across the country to want to play football.

The last time England reached a European Championship final was 2009 and that had ended in a 6-2 defeat to Germany. England also made the World Cup semi-finals in 2015 and 2019 but were yet to win a major tournament. Playing in the Euros 2022 was going to bring an whole new world of pressure and competition. But Leah was determined to face it all head on. She wanted to take her team and her country all the way to the trophy.

As the hosts, England were playing in Group A. Their opponents were going to be Austria, Norway and

Northern Ireland. They made a winning start by beating Austria 1-0 at a sold-out Old Trafford. Millie Bright and Leah were crucial in the win, but it was Mead who really made the difference, flicking the ball narrowly over the line to give England a first-half lead, and win the match.

Next up was a match against Norway. The Lionesses battered and bruised the opposition, putting eight goals past a team that had been tipped by many to go the distance at the Euros. An outstanding hat-trick from Mead stole the game, but it was an equally proud night for Leah.

The game broke the record for the most goals scored in a European Championship game. The Lionesses had sent a warning shot out to everyone in the competition. They were here to win.

Leah wanted her team to finish on a high before the knock-out stages. And they did exactly that. England finished their group stage off with a perfect record. They defeated Northern Ireland at St Mary's in Southampton, 5-0, with individual

goals from Fran Kirby and Mead, two goals from Alessia Russo, plus an unfortunate own goal from Northern Ireland's Kelsie Burrows.

England then faced off against Spain in the quarter final. Both sides wanted to win and played incredibly well. The score was 1-1 at the end of ninety minutes and had to go into extra time. Georgia Stanway saved the day for England, with a stunning strike that rocketed into the back of the net. The Lionesses were through to the next round.

Sweden were England's opposition

for the semi-final. This was a team that had enjoyed years of success in the women's game. But England had no intention of letting them repeat their success at Euro 2022.

The Lionesses thrashed the Swedes with a score of 4-0 in front of a jubilant crowd at Bramall Lane, Sheffield. It was all thanks to goals from Mead, Lucy Bronze, Kirby and an outrageous backheel from Russo.

A goal so good, that some now call a backheel nutmeg in that fashion *The Russo*!

England had done it; they had made it all the way to the final of Euro 2022. And Leah wanted to make sure that every single player felt proud of what they had achieved. They had pulled together and pushed themselves through hard work, determination and grit to the last day of the tournament.

'Everybody today was absolutely incredible and delivered what they needed to,' said Leah. 'This is what the team is about. At two opposite ends of the pitch everybody is making it count.'

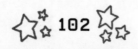

With the eyes of the footballing world on her, Leah wanted more than anything to win, and for The Lionesses to leave a legacy for every woman and girl.

# 12
# THE FINAL

On the day of the final, Leah led her team out of the tunnel and into the Wembley stadium. It was England vs Germany, and the record-breaking crowd cheered and applauded as their newfound heroes walked onto the pitch. The players stood tall for the national anthem and sang as loudly

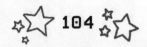

as they could in unison with the tens of thousands in support. 17 million people in England had tuned into watch the nail-biting win. And that didn't even count the crowds spilling out of pub doors, eyes glued to their screens. There was no doubt that the whole nation had fallen head over heels in love with The Lionesses.

The players got into position. Leah was at the back, focussing on the football delicately balanced on the centre spot, as the referee brought the whistle to her mouth. It was time for the UEFA Women's Euro 2022 Final.

A tense ninety minutes followed with flying tackles and yellow cards peppering a highly energetic game. In the 25th minute, Germany went close. The ball was swung into the box from a corner and it rebounded in the penalty area. It was only a handful of centimetres away from crossing the line, but Leah calmly blocked the ball from going over. With England's goalkeeper, Mary Earps, grabbing hold of the loose ball and clutching it tightly. At half-time the score was a nail-biting 0-0.

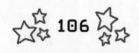

The Lionesses came out roaring into the second half and in the 62nd minute they created an incredible opportunity. Walsh played a pinpoint through ball over the German midfield and defence. Ella Toone ran past the defenders and latched onto the ball. It was now Toone vs Merle Frohms, the German goalkeeper.

Toone brought the ball under her control, while the goalkeeper ran off her line to put her under pressure. Toone dinked the ball over the head of the onrushing goalkeeper, and as it looped down and fell into the net the stadium erupted with cheers. It was happening. England were winning in the final! All they needed to do now was hold onto the lead.

Suddenly, without thinking, Leah glanced at the clock. This was something she avoided doing as she had a superstition that whenever she looked at the time in a match the other team would score. Shortly after she glanced at the clock, Germany scored. Tabea Waßmuth got in behind the England defence and fired a cross into the box.

Lina Magull was the first to reach the ball and using her left boot she fired an equaliser over the outstretched gloves of Earps.

Leah was furious at herself. She told herself this was a silly superstition and nothing more. Looking at the time hadn't caused this equaliser and she needed to be there for her team. Pulling herself together, she focused everything she had on the game. For a moment after the goal the crowd fell silent, but this wasn't the time to give up. Leah picked up her teammates and tried to inspire them. Neither side

could score the winning goal in ninety minutes, so the match went to extra time.

In just thirty minutes of extra playing time, the world would know the winners. And if no one scored in extra time, the match would go on to penalties.

Fans in the stadium could hardly watch as the match went into extra time and fans all over the world were staring anxiously at screens. Their nerves frayed as the final tense minutes of the match unfolded. But thanks to Wiegman's and Leah's words of encouragement, the England players remained calm and focused on the pitch. This was the time for confidence and belief. A belief that if a chance came along the team could take it.

In the 110th minute off the match, only ten minutes away from a potential penalty shootout, the ball dropped into the penalty box. It fell close to Chloe Kelly, the England striker, who stretched for the ball. The studs of her boots grazed it, but she was unable to bring it under her control. Yet luck was on her side, and the ball rebounded off a defender's leg giving her a second chance. Kelly prodded the ball into the net. Kelly ran out of the box, took off her top and waved it in the air. The stadium erupted with cheers that boomed across the nation. Fans released pure joy, excitement and relief at the top of their lungs as they realised what was happening. They were actually going to do it. The Lionesses were going to win!

As the referee blew her whistle and brought the match to a close, the Lionesses dropped to their knees.

England were champions. They had not only won the trophy, but they also inspired millions in the process.

As always, Leah looked for her family in the crowd so she could share the phenomenal feeling. Each of The Lionesses were handed their winning medals and took their spot on the presentation stand. Leah was the last one in the line, as she wouldn't just be receiving a medal, she would be given the trophy to lift too. Leah collected the trophy 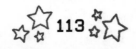 and walked to the front of the team as the fans started to cheer in anticipation. Wanting to share the moment, Leah asked her vice-captain Bright to lift the trophy with her. An England captain had not lifted a Euro or World Cup trophy since Alf Ramsey in 1966. History was being made, right here, right now. In front of the cheering crowd, Leah and Millie lifted the trophy into the air. White and red confetti fired out of cannons around them while the players and fans celebrated their victory, singing *Sweet Caroline* at the top of their voices.

This was a new beginning for women's football. England had hosted an incredible tournament, had changed the game in this country and hopefully across Europe and the rest of the world. Leah held the trophy in one hand, and the nations' hearts in the other.

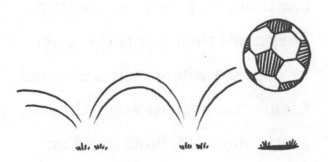

# 13
# PARTY TIME!

After the final whistle had blown
and the thousands in attendance
had left the stadium, there was only
one thing the players wanted to do.
They made their way to the lower
row of seats where their family and
friends had been waiting. Almost
every mum, dad, brother, sister,

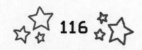

aunt, uncle, cousin, grandmother, grandfather and friend were wiping away tears of pride and joy. Leah hugged all of her close friends and family, knowing she would never have made it to this unbelievable moment without them.

After the trophy ceremony, Wiegman was asked to give a post-match press conference. But Leah and the rest of The Lionesses weren't going to let her do it quietly. They burst into the press conference singing, dancing and jumping around behind their manager.

'I can't stop crying,' Leah told the BBC. 'We talk and we talk and we've finally done it.' It was truly the proudest moment of her life. She, Wiegman and the rest of the team had brought people together and got them to games. 'This is just the start of the journey,' she promised.

In the dressing room, the match's sports drinks were swapped for champagne. Some of the girls' favourite songs by artists such as ABBA and Céline Dion – not to forget *Sweet Caroline* and *Freed From Desire* – blasted through speakers as

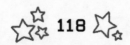

everyone sang and danced along. The UEFA Women's Euros 2022 trophy sat proudly on the floor in the middle of it all.

The Lionesses had united the entire country during their campaign. Millions had tuned in to watch their matches throughout the tournament and the players had not only inspired a younger generation, but had shown the world just how exciting, thrilling and dramatic the women's game can be. The sport deserves not only a space in the spotlight, but continued support and a growing audience.

The next day, thousands of fans gathered under the sizzling summer sun for a party, waving England flags in the air as the entire Lioness team bounded on the specially built stage. The team had partied more than they had played football in the last twenty-four hours, but they weren't ready to stop anytime soon.

Draped in an England flag and wearing a red bucket hat, Leah made her way to the front of the stage and started to speak. 'The legacy of the tournament was already made before that final game,' she told the

 cheering crowd. 'What we've done for women and young girls that can look up and inspire to be us. I think England have hosted an incredible tournament and we've changed the game in this country and hopefully across the world.'

Leah also made sure that she thanked Wiegman. She told the cheering crowd that the manager was the missing ingredient that the team had been looking for, and just how much Wiegman had brought the team together.

Leah did her best to hide her emotion as she spotted hundreds of young girls clapping and cheering in the crowd. They would never have to think twice about their right to play football.

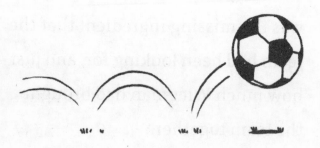

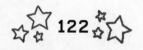

# 14
# THE FUTURE

The next few months were a whirlwind for Leah and her teammates. Leah had been catapulted into the public eye and reached a new level of fame.

She was recognised wherever she goes. Fashion designers invited her to runway shows and regularly dressed her for appearances. It was a long way

from the cheap t-shirts she used to buy.

Fame isn't always a good thing, but Leah understood that fame is a part of football, and she was still thankful to all the women players who came before her and paved the way.

'If you're not prepared to be famous, you're doing a disservice to the game and all those women who had to pretend to be boys to be able to play,' she said, in an interview when reflecting over her fame. 'I understand that I stand on the shoulders of those people.'

Success and fame won't change

Leah. In fact, she says she will be chasing the feeling of winning the Euros for the rest of her life. There's only one small thing that Leah wishes she could make happen. She'd love to go back and watch the Euro finals from the stands with her family.

One thing's for sure, Leah may be one of the greatest footballers of our time, but her feet are firmly on the ground. Her most recent New Year resolutions were tidying up after herself, taking more time for herself and keeping a diary to organise herself. Unbelievably, she's still training as an accountant in case her football career fails. Just as she had been as the nervous teenager studying for her GCSEs. Often wondering what her future career would look like.

And of course, Leah wants to make sure that the world treats women footballers with the respect they deserve. As part of that, The Lionesses have set up their *Let Girls Play* campaign – the brainchild of Leah's teammate Lotte Wubben-Moy. The goal is to give girls the same opportunities in football as boys.

Leah believes that this campaign will change things for future players who may not even be born yet. 'There must be an opportunity for every single girl to play football if they want to,' she says.

More than anything Leah wants to see a world where girls can be what they want to be. That both girls and boys know that women can do whatever they want. No one should ever be treated differently because of their gender.

And of course, there's one more trophy that Leah would love to get

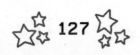

her hands on; the World Cup trophy. The Lionesses will be participating in the 2023 World Cup being held in Australia and New Zealand. With an increased fan base, millions will be watching The Lionesses take on the rest of the world.

Thanks to Leah, women's football is finally getting its shot on the main stage.